Common Core Lessons & Activities:

The Bill of Rights

By Carole Marsh

Published by Gallopade International, Inc.

Printed in the U.S.A. (Peachtree City, Georgia)

TABLE OF CONTENTS

G: Includes Graphic Organizer

GO: Graphic Organizer is also available 8½" x
download at www.gallopade.com/client/
(numbers above correspond to the grap

I0895168

READING INFORMATIONAL TEXT

Father of the Bill of Rights

Read the text and answer the questions.

George Mason did not particularly like politics, but he believed strongly in individual freedoms. When Britain began to unfairly tax the colonies before the American Revolution, George Mason got involved. He took George Washington's position in the Virginia Legislature so Washington could lead the Continental Army.

After the thirteen colonies declared their independence from Great Britain during the Revolutionary War, the new states began writing their state constitutions. George Mason wrote the Virginia Constitution. He also wrote the Virginia Declaration of Rights to protect the individual rights of Virginians. Other states soon did the same thing.

In 1787, the U.S Constitution replaced the old Articles of Confederation. The Articles had given the states a lot of power but gave little power to the federal government. Because of that, running the new government was difficult. To fix this problem, the new Constitution gave more power to the federal government.

As a result, George Mason urged his fellow delegates to add a bill of rights to the Constitution to protect individual freedoms. Many delegates did not agree. They argued that individual rights were already protected under state constitutions. Adding one to the U.S. Constitution seemed unnecessary.

To protest, George Mason refused to sign the Constitution. He argued that federal laws would <u>supersede</u> those of the states, taking away some rights of states and citizens. Two states, Rhode Island and North Carolina also refused to ratify the Constitution without a bill of rights. After much debate, the states agreed to sign the Constitution on the condition that a bill of rights was added later.

As promised, James Madison drafted a bill of rights during the first Congress. He borrowed ideas from George Mason's Virginia Declaration of Rights. The U.S. Constitution was amended to include the Bill of Rights (Amendments I-X) in December 1791. George Mason is honored with the title of "Father of the Bill of Rights" for his many contributions.

PART A: Use the text to infer whether each statement is **true** or **false**. Write **T** for true and **F** for false. Correct the false statements.

1. ______ George Mason served a minor role in the Virginia Legislature.
2. ______ George Mason wrote the Virginia Declaration of Independence.
3. ______ The purpose of a bill of rights is to protect individual rights and freedoms.
4. ______ Some states refused to ratify the U.S. Constitution without a bill of rights.
5. ______ George Mason was influenced by James Madison's ideas when he wrote a draft of the Bill of Rights.

PART B: Read the following quotation and explain how it supports George Mason's opinion about a bill of rights.

6. Excerpt from a letter to James Madison, concerning the lack of a bill of rights in the Constitution: "*...a bill of rights is what the people are entitled to against every government on earth...and what no just government should refuse...*" —Thomas Jefferson, December 1787

PART C: Answer the following questions about the text.

7. Explain how the Articles of Confederation and the new Constitution differed. What did this prompt George Mason to do? Explain why.
8. Some delegates argued that the U.S. Constitution did not need a bill of rights. What arguments did they use?
9. Define <u>supersede</u> as it is used in the text. Rewrite the sentence in the text using a synonym for supersede.
10. Cite two ways George Mason showed his disapproval when convention delegates refused to add a bill of rights to the Constitution.
11. Cite evidence from the text that supports the claim that George Mason is the "Father of the Bill of Rights."

BONUS: Write an "If" poem that begins: "If George Mason hadn't replaced George Washington in the Virginia Legislature, George Mason wouldn't have written the Virginia Declaration of Rights. If he hadn't written the Virginia Declaration of Rights, ..."

John Locke's Influence

Read the text and answer the questions.

The idea that individual rights should be protected by law has its roots in the theories of early 17th century philosopher John Locke. Locke wrote that people should be free to do as they please, as long as they do not hurt others. He stated that all men are created equal and have the right to defend their rights to "life, health, liberty, or possessions."

John Locke argued that people will willingly give up some freedoms to form a government to protect these natural rights to life, liberty, and property. This agreement among the people to live under a set of laws is called a social contract.

The founding fathers drew from these early lessons in philosophy when writing social contracts, such as the Declaration of Independence, the U.S. Constitution, and the Bill of Rights.

1. Use an online dictionary to define philosopher.
2. John Locke stated that all men are created equal and have the right to defend their rights to "life, health, liberty, or possessions." Explain what John Locke meant by this statement.
3. Use the text to write a definition of social contract. Infer what freedoms people give up when they form social contracts. Predict what would happen if people did not form social contracts.
4. Explain how the Bill of Rights is a social contract.
5. On a separate sheet of paper, create a Venn diagram (see below) to compare and contrast John Locke's philosophy and the Bill of Rights. Use the text here and a copy of the Bill of Rights.

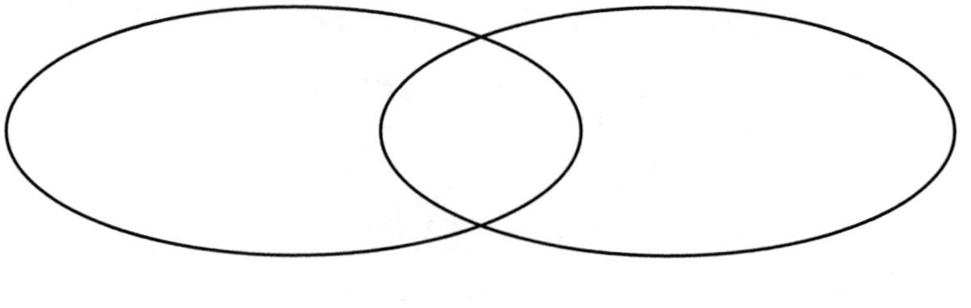

Amending the Constitution

Use the text and the flowchart to answer the questions.

Changes to the Constitution are called amendments. At the first Federal Congress in 1789, James Madison proposed to amend, or change, the brand-new Constitution to better protect individual rights. His proposal was debated in both houses of Congress. In the end, both Houses voted and agreed to send twelve proposed amendments to the state legislatures for ratification. The states ratified ten of them. These are known as the Bill of Rights.

Process to Amend the U.S. Constitution

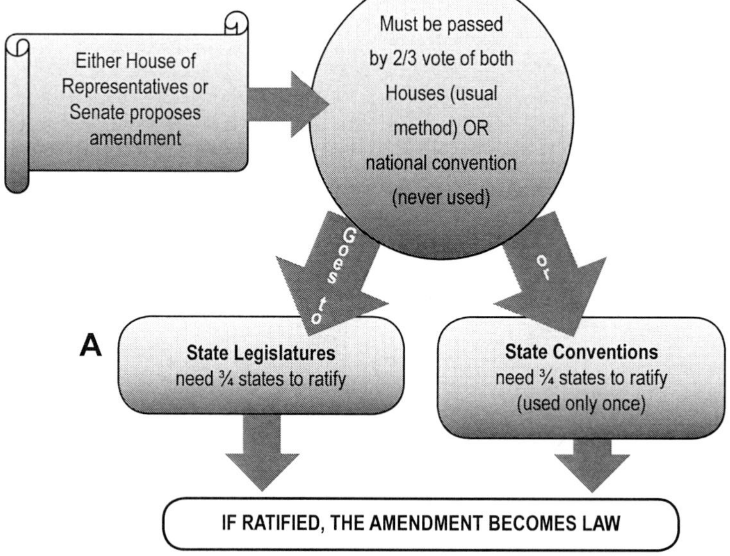

1. What is the first step in amending the Constitution?
2. In order for a proposed amendment to be passed on to the states for ratification, what must happen first?
3. Use evidence from the text and flowchart to determine where (either A or B) the Bill of Rights amendments were debated and ratified.
4. Cite evidence to support the statement, "Amending the Constitution is a difficult process."

Rights and Limitations

The first ten amendments to the Constitution, also known as the Bill of Rights, were designed to protect individual rights and freedoms, while at the same time limiting the government's use of its power. The amendments are explained (paraphrased) below.

Read the summary of each amendment. Identify the main individual freedoms and/or limitations on government, and write them as they impact you on the graphic organizer. One amendment has been completed as an example.

I. Congress cannot make laws that limit a person's freedom of religion, freedom of speech, freedom to publish what he wants to, right to demonstrate peacefully with others, or right to ask the government to change something he doesn't like.

II. The government cannot take away the right of a person to carry or use a weapon to defend himself.

III. During peacetime, Congress cannot force a person to board soldiers; in wartime, they have to pass a law first.

IV. Citizens have the right to feel safe in their homes. No one can search a person's home, body, or things without a search warrant.

V. A person cannot be charged with a serious crime unless a grand jury says there is enough evidence for a trial. If a jury decides a person is innocent of a crime, that person cannot be tried again with a different jury for the same crime. A person does not have to testify against himself unless he wants to confess.

VI. A person who is arrested for a crime has the right to a speedy and public trial, with a jury of people in the area. A person has the right to know what he is accused of and who is testifying against him. A person has the right to a lawyer, even if he can't afford one.

VII. A person has the right to a jury trial in a federal civil case.

VIII. The government must not set unreasonable bail. When a person commits a crime, the punishment should not be cruel or unusual.

IX. People have rights, even the ones not listed in the Constitution.

X. In the Constitution, the powers that are not granted to the government are given to the states, or to the people.

#	Rights & Freedoms / Limitations on Government
I	
II	
III	
IV	I have the right to feel safe in my home. The government can't search my home without a warrant.
V	
VI	
VII	
VIII	
IX	
X	

1. Write a short essay explaining the purpose of the Bill of Rights?
2. As a class, debate which amendments are the most and least applicable to you. Discuss how your opinion might change as you get older.

READING INFORMATIONAL TEXT

The First Amendment

The First Amendment to the U.S. Constitution guarantees protection of five individual rights. It also limits the government from making laws that infringe upon those rights.

Read the texts and answer the questions.

The First Amendment

"Congress shall make no law respecting an establishment of religion, or prohibiting the free exercise thereof; or abridging the freedom of speech, or of the press; or the right of the people peaceably to assemble, and to petition the government for a redress of grievances."

Most Supreme Court justices have agreed that the First Amendment is not without limits. Although the First Amendment protects the right to free speech, it does not protect speech that is untruthful, false, or dangerous to the security of the government. To summarize, the First Amendment has limitations on writing and saying things that are harmful to others; these are known as libel and slander. In addition, the First Amendment does not protect violent or forceful assembly.

1. List the five rights protected by the First Amendment.
2. Using evidence from the text, define libel and slander. Give two examples that highlight the difference between the two words.
3. The First Amendment says that Congress cannot make laws that abridge, or limit, the freedom of speech. Does this mean that you can say anything you want any time you want? Write a short response, and use evidence from the text to support your argument.
4. What word in the First Amendment limits the people's right to assemble?
5. List the First Amendment rights in order of importance to you. Compare your list with other students' lists and discuss.

March on Washington

In the 1960s, many African Americans and white Americans urged President Kennedy and Congress to make a law that would guarantee equal rights and quality education for African Americans. In 1963, more than 250,000 people gathered in Washington, D.C., to assert their First Amendment rights and get Congress' attention! This March on Washington sent a clear message to Congress to vote "Yes!" on civil rights legislation.

Look at the photo from the March on Washington and answer the questions.

Courtesy of National Archives

1. What First Amendment rights did the March on Washington demonstrate?
2. How has the First Amendment been important to the Civil Rights Movement?
3. Is the right to free speech important today? Give an oral report predicting what would happen if the right to free speech were taken away.
4. Why did protesters choose to march on Washington, D.C., instead of another city?

The Second Amendment

The Second Amendment to the U.S. Constitution guarantees protection of people's right to keep and bear arms.

Read the text and answer the questions.

The Second Amendment

A well regulated militia being necessary to the security of a free state, the right of the people to keep and bear arms shall not be infringed.

1. Use a dictionary to define the following terms as they are used in the Second Amendment.
   A. militia
   B. keep
   C. bear
   D. arms
   E. infringed
2. Well regulated means "well trained." Why do you think the authors of the Second Amendment chose to write "a well regulated militia" as opposed to "a militia"?
3. According to the Second Amendment, what was the purpose for maintaining a well-regulated militia?
4. Use evidence from the text to support the statement, "The Second Amendment *protects* the right to keep and bear arms."
5. The right to own and bear arms was important to the first colonists and settlers who moved west. What reasons might early settlers have had to bear arms? Use an online resource to gather information.

BONUS: Create a graphic organizer to display the pros and cons of the Second Amendment.

PROBLEM-SOLUTION-RESULTS

The Third Amendment

Read the texts and answer the questions. Then use the texts to complete the Problem-Solution organizer.

The Third Amendment

No Soldier shall, in time of peace be quartered in any house, without the consent of the Owner, nor in time of war, but in a manner to be prescribed by law.

The Third Amendment may seem unusual now, but when this amendment was written, soldiers would often stay in nearby homes. When the colonies were under British rule, Britain passed laws that forced American colonists to feed and find housing (empty barns, inns, bars) for the British troops. Later, the king enacted the Quartering Act of 1774 (one of the Intolerable Acts) to punish the American colonists for dumping British tea into Boston Harbor. The Act forced American colonists to quarter British troops—even in private homes! Not only was it a hardship to feed and house these troops, the colonists felt their privacy was being violated.

1. Use a dictionary to define quartered as it is used in the Third Amendment.
2. What can you infer about the colonists' opinion of the Quartering Act of 1774? Cite evidence to support your conclusion.
3. Recreate the graphic organizer on a separate sheet of paper. Use information from the text to identify the problems, solutions, and results of the Third Amendment.

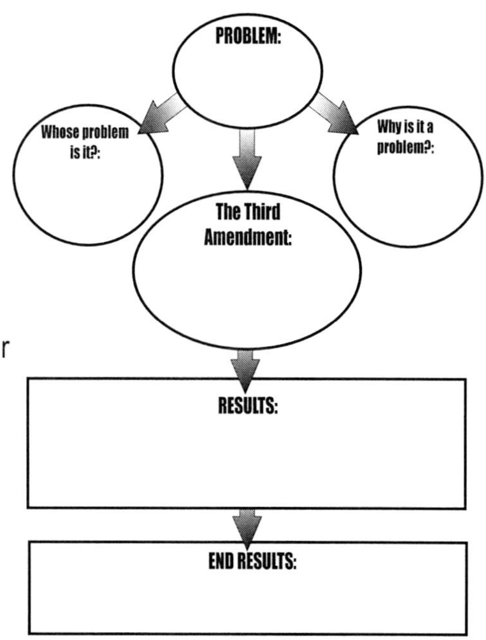

The Bill of Rights

In your own words, summarize what rights are granted or protected by each Bill of Rights amendment. One amendment has been filled in for you as an example.

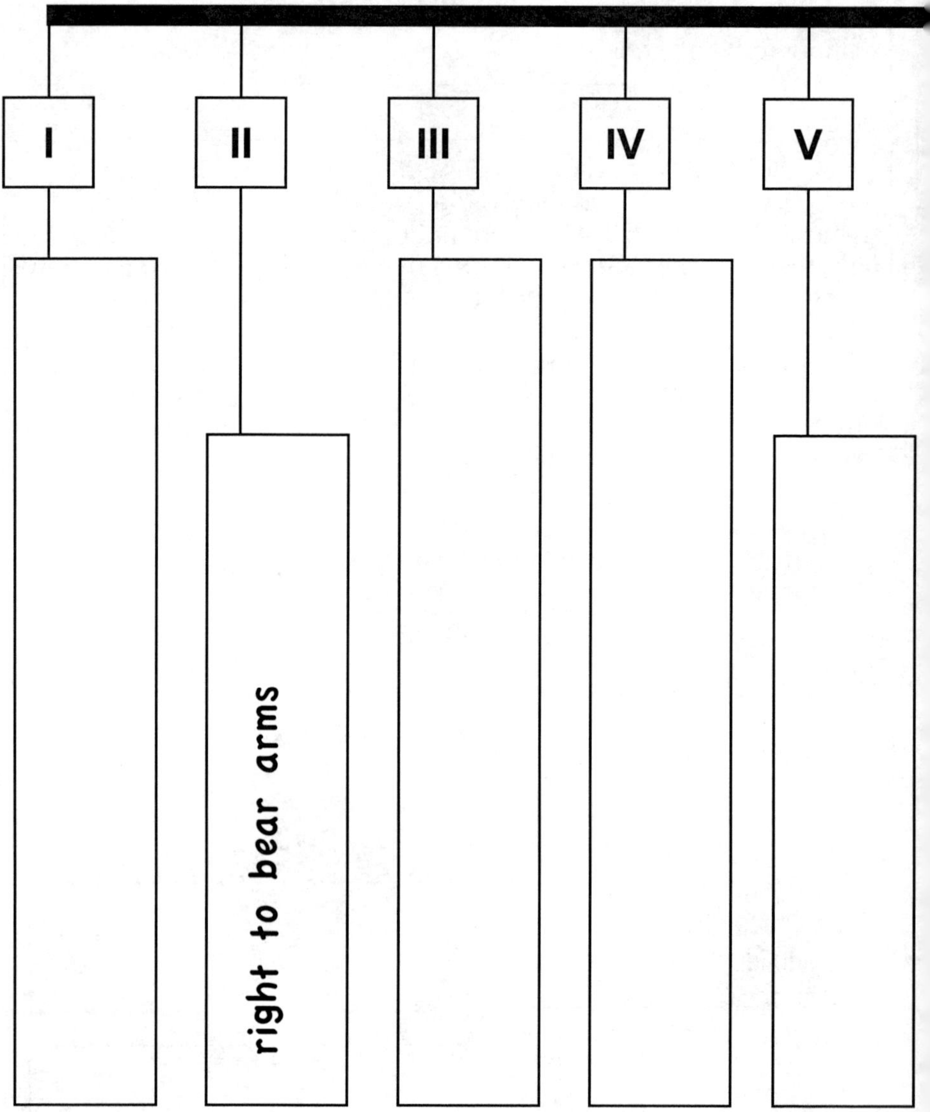

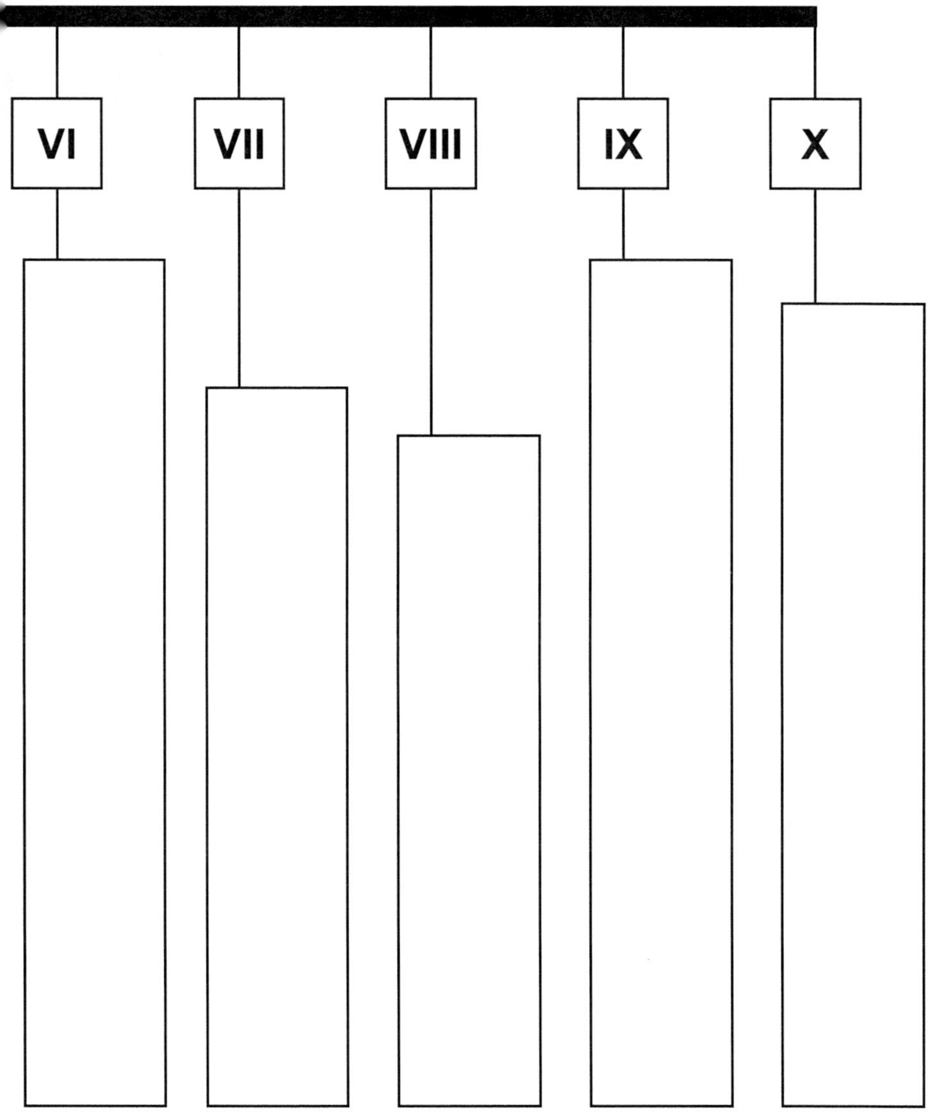
VI
VII
VIII
IX
X

The Fourth Amendment

The Fourth Amendment protects a person against unlawful searches and seizures. The following is a Supreme Court case involving the Fourth Amendment.

Read the text and answer the questions.

The Fourth Amendment protects our privacy. It states, "The right of the people to be secure in their persons, houses, papers, and effects, against unreasonable searches and seizures, shall not be violated, and no Warrants shall issue, but upon probable cause, supported by Oath or affirmation, and particularly describing the place to be searched, and the persons or things to be seized."

The 1927 Supreme Court case *Olmstead v. United States* involved a man by the name of Roy Olmstead. He was suspected of smuggling and selling alcohol during Prohibition, a time when it was against the law to distribute, make, and sell alcohol.

To gather evidence against Mr. Olmstead, police wiretapped his office phone without a warrant, or lawful permission. The Supreme Court ruled 5-4 that use of the evidence was allowable. Supreme Court Chief Justice Taft argued that wiretapping was not the same as a physical search and seizure as stated in the Fourth Amendment.

Supreme Court Justice Brandeis disagreed with the ruling. He argued that wiretapping is just as intrusive as opening someone's mail without permission. He supported his argument by citing how the Fourth Amendment protected a person's right to privacy.

1. A. Use an online dictionary to define intrusive.
   B. Wiretapping is the act of monitoring or recording a phone call without permission. Explain how wiretapping is intrusive.
2. Rewrite the Fourth Amendment in your own words.
3. How did the Fourth Amendment apply in the Olmstead case? Cite evidence from the text to support the relationship.
4. In your opinion, why is the Fourth Amendment important? Write a two paragraph response explaining why the Fourth Amendment is important and predicting what might happen if the Fourth Amendment did not protect individuals from unlawful searches and seizures.

The Fifth Amendment

The Fifth Amendment makes sure that the rights of the accused are protected in the criminal justice system. A person accused of a crime has the right to 1) know his/her rights 2) receive due process, a fair trial by jury after evidence is collected 3) not be charged with the same crime twice 4) have a lawyer present during questioning.

Read the text and answer the questions.

In 1963, Ernesto Miranda was accused of a brutal crime and arrested. Police questioned him without first telling him his rights. Police used a signed confession to find him guilty in a court of law.

His lawyer tried to have the confession thrown out as evidence because he felt that police broke the law by failing to tell Mr. Miranda that he 1) didn't have to say anything that might be self-incriminating, and 2) had the right to an attorney during questioning. The lower court threw out Miranda's attorney's motion, or request, and allowed the confession as evidence in court.

The case was appealed to the Supreme Court. In *Miranda v. Arizona,* the Supreme Court agreed with Miranda's lawyer. The Court ruled that the confession could *not* be used as evidence, since Mr. Miranda was not told his rights before questioning.

Now, to better protect the rights of the accused, police are required to give a Miranda warning before questioning a person accused of a crime.

1. Use a dictionary to explain the difference between the meanings of incriminating and self-incriminating. Which type of testimony is limited by the Fifth Amendment?
2. Who do you have a right to have present when questioned by police?
3. When a trial is not fair, or due process is not followed, the case can be appealed. Explain the meaning of appealed as it is used in the text.
4. Explain how the Fifth Amendment protected Mr. Miranda.
5. What are all police required to do as a result of the *Miranda v. Arizona* Supreme Court decision? What is the purpose of this requirement?

PRIMARY SOURCE ANALYSIS

The Fifth Amendment

This political cartoon was drawn in the early 20th century. It shows Lady Justice riding on a snail.

Analyze the cartoon and answer the questions.

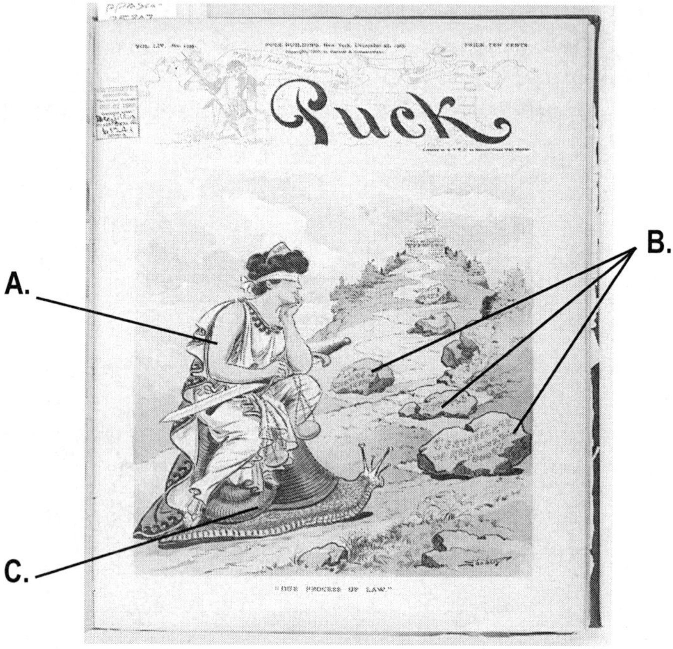

1. Identify what is symbolized in the cartoon.
   A. What is represented by the person marked by arrow A?
   B. What is represented by the objects marked by arrows B?
   C. What is represented by the object marked by arrow C?
2. What would you title this cartoon?
3. What is the cartoonist's opinion of "Due Process of Law"? What symbols or images support your conclusion?
4. Why might the artist have depicted Lady Justice wearing a blindfold?
5. Discuss the political cartoon as a class. Expand your answers and compose a typed report explaining the main idea.

PRIMARY SOURCE ANALYSIS

The Sixth Amendment

Read the text. Match the numbered phrases with their explanations in the chart.

The Sixth Amendment

In all criminal prosecutions, the accused shall enjoy the 1) right to a speedy and 2) public trial, by an 3) impartial jury of the 4) state and district wherein the crime shall have been committed, which district shall have been previously ascertained by law, and 5) to be informed of the nature and cause of the accusation; 6) to be confronted with the witnesses against him; 7) to have a required process for obtaining witnesses in his favor, and 8) to have the assistance of counsel for his defense.

#	**Explanation**
	Jurors must be unbiased, and will decide guilt or innocence based on evidence presented at the trial.
	Defendant has the right to know what he/she is accused of.
	Defendant has the right to not wait long in jail before the trial takes place.
	The trial must be held in a public court, not a secret location.
	Defendant has the right to know who his/her accuser is.
	The trial location will be held in the area where the crime took place.
	Defendant has the right to a lawyer, even if he/she cannot afford to pay for the lawyer's services.
	Defendant has the right to call witnesses to testify for his/her benefit.

READING INFORMATIONAL TEXT

The Seventh Amendment

Criminal cases are protected by the Sixth Amendment, but civil cases, non-criminal cases, involving money from business, property, etc., are protected by the Seventh Amendment. A person seeking damages (money, property, etc.) from a defendant has the right to a jury trial in a federal court.

Read the text and answer the questions.

When the colonies were still controlled by Great Britain, colonists were not allowed to have a jury trial. Judges alone made decisions in civil trials. The judges were often corrupt and ruled unfairly. The Seventh Amendment, protecting the right to a jury trial in certain civil cases, protects people from this kind of abuse of power.

If the money involved in a case is more than a certain amount, a jury trial in federal court may be requested. First, though, the judge will encourage the parties involved to settle out of court due to the cost of a trial. If a settlement can't be reached, a jury trial can be scheduled.

The job of a judge in the jury trial is not to make the final decision, but to instruct the jury on the law and evidence that can be used. The jury decides if there is enough evidence. The jury then hands down a verdict and can award money in damages.

1. Use a dictionary to define jury trial as it is used in the text.
2. According to the text, why would a judge encourage two parties to settle an argument without a court trial?
3. Explain the relationship between the Sixth and Seventh Amendments. What is the difference between a civil trial and a criminal trial?
4. According to the text, what aspects of British control caused colonists to create the Seventh Amendment?
5. Compare and contrast the roles of the judge and the jury in a jury trial. What are the pros and cons of having a jury make decisions instead of a judge?

PRIMARY SOURCE ANALYSIS

The Eighth Amendment

Read the text, look at the illustration, and answer the questions.

The Eighth Amendment

Excessive bail shall not be required, nor excessive fines imposed, nor cruel and unusual punishments inflicted.

The cartoon shows a British colonial pillory, a form of public punishment.

1. Bail is a sum of money required for release from jail. What limitation does the Eighth Amendment put on bail? Why was this done?
2. Define cruel and unusual punishments in your own words.
3. Explain how using a pillory stock could be considered cruel and unusual punishment. Cite details from the illustration.
4. Like many of the Bill of Rights amendments, the Eighth Amendment was written to avoid some of the problems that existed during colonial times. Based on this statement, use the Eighth Amendment to make three inferences about the legal system when the colonies were ruled by Britain.

Ninth & Tenth Amendments

Amendments nine and ten of the Bill of Rights limit the power of the federal government and protect the rights not specifically listed in the Constitution.

Define the underlined words. Then complete the graphic organizer by using the chart to rewrite the amendments in your own words.

1. Use a dictionary to define the following words: enumeration, construed, deny, disparage, and retained.

The Ninth Amendment	Meaning
The enumeration in the Constitution, of certain rights, →	
shall not be construed to deny or disparage others retained by the people. →	

What the amendment means to me:

2. Use a dictionary to define the following words: delegated, prohibited, and reserved.

The Tenth Amendment	Meaning
The powers not delegated to the United States by the Constitution,	
nor prohibited by it to the States	
are reserved to the States respectively, or to the people.	

What the amendment means to me:

3. Compare and contrast the Ninth and Tenth Amendments. What is the purpose of each? Compare your response with a partner.

4. Many delegates at the constitutional convention were against the Bill of Rights. They worried that by listing certain rights they would limit others. In your opinion, does the Bill of Rights limit other rights? Why or why not?

Bill of Rights Vocabulary

Complete the graphic organizer for each expression.
Bonus: Identify the amendment associated with each term.

Vocabulary:

double jeopardy	free speech	cruel & unusual punishment
search and seizure	due process	speedy and public trial
freedom of religion	trial by jury	right to bear arms

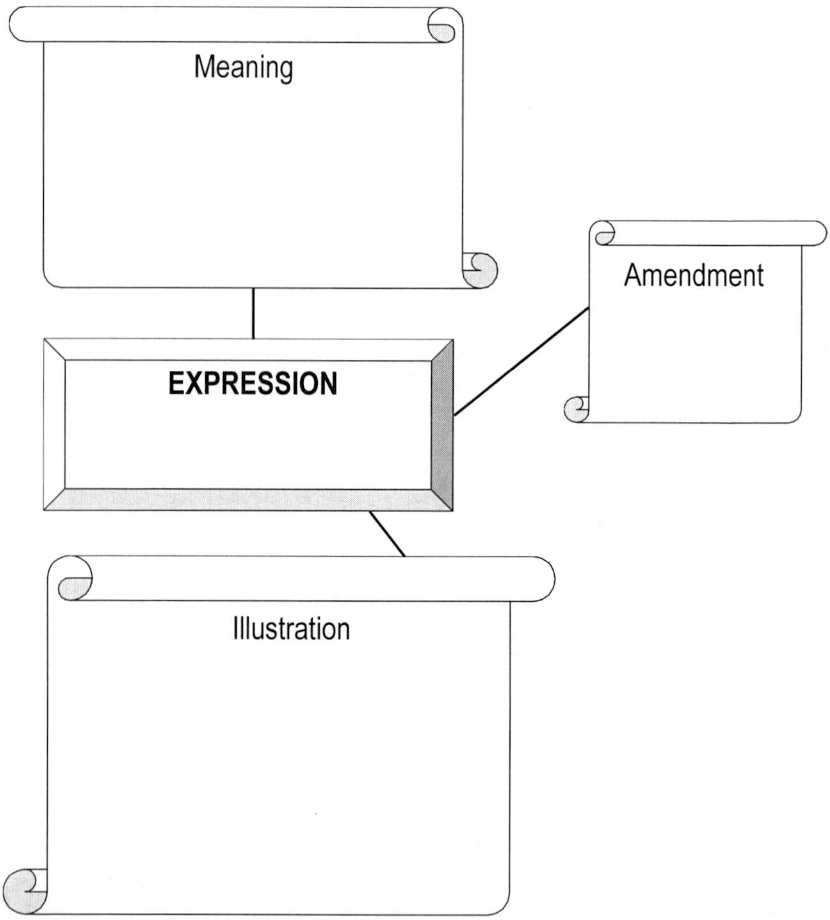

Four Freedoms

This poster is a graphical depiction of President Franklin D. Roosevelt's "Four Freedoms" Speech given just before the United States became involved in World War II.

Look at the poster and answer the questions.

Courtesy of Library of Congress

1. List the four freedoms highlighted by Franklin Roosevelt's Four Freedoms speech. Explain what each of these freedoms means.
2. What conclusions can you make based on the visual representations of the Four Freedoms of 1941 as related to the First Amendment Freedoms of 1791?
3. What is the significance of the phrase "Everywhere in the World"?
4. Who was the audience, and what was the purpose of this poster?
5. Describe how you might have reacted to this poster in 1941. Explain your response.

Correlations to Common Core State Standards

For your convenience, correlations are listed page-by-page, and for the entire book!

This book is correlated to the Common Core State Standards for English Language Arts grades 3-8, and to Common Core State Standards for Literacy in History, Science, & Technological Subjects grades 6-8.

Correlations are highlighted in gray.

PAGE #	READING *Includes:* RI: Reading Informational Text RH: Reading History	WRITING *Includes:* W: Writing WHST: Writing History, Science, & Technology	LANGUAGE *Includes:* L: Language LF: Language Foundational Skills	SPEAKING & LISTENING *Includes:* SL: Speaking & Listening
2-3	RI RH **1 2** 3 **4** 5 **6** 7 8 **9 10**	W WHST 1 2 3 4 5 6 7 8 9 10	L LF 1 2 3 **4** 5 **6**	SL 1 2 3 4 5 6
4	RI RH **1 2** 3 **4** 5 **6** 7 8 9 **10**	W WHST 1 2 3 4 5 6 7 **8 9 10**	L LF 1 2 3 **4** 5 **6**	SL 1 2 3 4 5 6
5	RI RH 1 2 **3** 4 5 6 7 8 9 **10**	W WHST 1 2 3 4 5 6 7 8 9 10	L LF 1 2 3 4 5 6	SL 1 2 3 4 5 6
6-7	RI RH **1 2** 3 **4** 5 6 7 8 9 **10**	W WHST **1** 2 3 4 5 6 7 8 9 **10**	L LF 1 2 3 4 5 6	SL **1** 2 3 4 5 **6**
8	RI RH **1 2** 3 **4** 5 6 7 8 9 **10**	W WHST 1 **2** 3 4 5 6 7 8 9 **10**	L LF 1 2 3 **4** 5 **6**	SL **1** 2 3 **4** 5 **6**
9	RI RH **1 2** 3 4 5 **6** 7 8 9 **10**	W WHST 1 2 3 4 5 6 7 8 9 10	L LF 1 2 3 4 5 6	SL 1 2 3 4 5 6
10	RI RH **1 2 3 4 5 6** 7 8 9 **10**	W WHST 1 2 3 4 5 6 **7 8** 9 **10**	L LF 1 2 3 **4** 5 **6**	SL 1 2 3 4 5 6
11	RI RH **1 2** 3 4 5 6 **7 8** 9 **10**	W WHST 1 2 3 4 5 6 7 8 9 10	L LF 1 2 3 4 5 6	SL **1** 2 3 4 5 **6**
12-13	RI RH **1 2** 3 4 5 6 7 8 9 **10**	W WHST 1 2 3 4 5 6 7 8 9 10	L LF 1 2 3 4 5 6	SL 1 2 3 4 5 6
14	RI RH **1 2 3 4** 5 6 7 8 9 **10**	W WHST **1 2** 3 4 5 6 7 **8** 9 **10**	L LF 1 2 3 **4** 5 **6**	SL 1 2 3 4 5 6
15	RI RH **1 2** 3 **4** 5 6 7 8 9 **10**	W WHST 1 2 3 4 5 **6** 7 8 9 **10**	L LF 1 2 3 **4** 5 **6**	SL 1 2 3 4 **5 6**
16	RI RH 1 2 3 4 5 6 **7 8** 9 **10**	W WHST 1 2 3 4 5 6 7 8 9 10	L LF 1 2 3 4 5 6	SL **1** 2 3 4 5 **6**
17	RI RH **1 2** 3 4 5 6 7 8 9 **10**	W WHST 1 2 3 4 5 6 7 8 9 10	L LF 1 2 3 4 5 6	SL 1 2 3 4 5 6
18	RI RH **1 2** 3 **4 5** 6 7 8 9 **10**	W WHST 1 2 3 4 5 6 7 8 9 10	L LF 1 2 3 **4** 5 **6**	SL 1 2 3 4 5 6
19	RI RH **1 2** 3 **4** 5 6 **7** 8 **9 10**	W WHST 1 2 3 4 5 6 7 8 9 10	L LF 1 2 3 4 5 6	SL 1 2 3 4 5 6
20	RI RH 1 2 3 **4** 5 6 7 8 9 **10**	W WHST 1 2 3 4 5 6 7 8 9 10	L LF 1 2 3 **4** 5 **6**	SL 1 2 3 4 5 6
21	RI RH **1 2** 3 **4** 5 6 7 8 9 10	W WHST 1 2 3 4 **5** 6 7 8 9 **10**	L LF 1 2 3 **4** 5 **6**	SL 1 2 3 4 5 6
22	RI RH **1 2** 3 **4** 5 6 7 8 9 **10**	W WHST 1 2 3 4 5 6 7 8 9 10	L LF 1 2 3 4 5 6	SL 1 2 3 4 5 6
23	RI RH **1 2** 3 4 5 6 **7** 8 9 **10**	W WHST 1 2 **3** 4 5 **6** 7 8 9 **10**	L LF 1 2 3 4 **5 6**	SL 1 2 3 4 5 6
COMPLETE BOOK	RI RH **1 2 3 4 5 6 7 8 9 10**	W WHST **1 2 3 4 5 6 7 8 9 10**	L LF 1 2 3 **4 5 6**	SL **1** 2 3 **4 5 6**

For the complete Common Core standard identifier, combine your grade + "." + letter code above + "." + number code above.

In addition to the correlations indicated here, the activities may be adapted or expanded to align to additional standards and to meet the diverse needs of your unique students!